The Beginners Guide to Becoming a Fire Fighter

Table of Contents

Introduction

I want to thank you and congratulate you for purchasing the book "The Beginners Guide to Becoming a Fire Fighter".

This book contains proven steps and strategies on how to become a firefighter in the U.S.

Here's an inescapable fact: in order to stand amongst the other candidates, you need to start preparing for the tests early and get some hands-on experience to compete better. This book will help you understand and prepare you to find out the best ways to increase your chances in order to get hired into a fire service.

If you do not learn the tips and tricks to help you prepare better, you may lose the opportunity to land your dream career at the fire department. It is time for you to hone up your skills and serve America. Downloading this book brings you one step closer to achieving your dream career with the fire service. Your purchase of this book demonstrates your will and enthusiasm to become a firefighter. There is fierce competition for firefighter jobs so preparation is going to be the key to landing the job.

Chapter 1: How to Become a Firefighter in the U.S.

Firefighters work in different places like the forests, suburbs or the metropolitan cities. If you want to become a firefighter you need to first find out the kind of service you are interested to join - federal, state, rural, regional, or city. Some jobs at the fire department may apply to a high school student whereas some may require an emergency medical technician (EMT) certification. Find out which path applies to you before prepare or apply for the job.

There are around 300,000 firefighter positions in the U.S. You will find most of these positions in the metropolitans where they have more sources of funding due to larger tax base. Smaller towns or communities may rely more on the volunteer firefighting services. Sometimes if there is expansion in the area, more funds can be provided for expanding the fire departments too. Attrition rate is pretty low and so is the hiring rate. The exams are held yearly most of the time. You may find public announcements in the local media several weeks ahead of the test. If you are serious about joining the fire service, it is better you fill up the application form now itself so that once the exam dates are finalized, you will be notified immediately by mail. That way you will not miss any exam. If you miss the chance, you may have to wait for another year. Typically, you will find the application forms at your local fire department or even the civil service bureau.

Your duties at the fire department will vary. Sometimes you may have to just perform mundane tasks like testing and keeping the fire equipment ready for any emergency. Sometimes you may have to work long hours under dangerous circumstances to provide rescue and relief. You may be exposed to hazardous conditions like smoke inhalation, carcinogenic materials, unstable buildings, falling debris, etc. You may have to perform salvaging operations like removing debris, transporting injured victims, sweep water, speak to schools about evacuation procedure, assist medical personnel in evaluating victims, etc.

Firefighters normally spend 24 hours on duty and 48 hours off duty. Some departments also have better shifts like 8-10 hour daily shifts. Under any circumstances you will typically spend 45 to 50 hours every week at work. In case you are on 24 hours shifts, you will be provided accommodation inside the fire department facility. So you will have access to kitchen, study, locker rooms, sleeping areas, bathrooms, etc. Amidst the shift you will also have access to games, technical reading and other fun activities. Just make sure you are ready to leave at the sound of an emergency.

New hires typically engage after 1 to 3 months of intense study and training. During this period they learn about how to use all the firefighting equipments and about fire technology. They may be allowed to demonstrate their skills but under the close supervision of a fire lieutenant.

Entry-level firefighters typically earn approximately $3,000 every month. This excludes overtime. If you are a fire lieutenant, you can expect around $3,700 every month. Battalion chiefs or anyone with a higher rank can receive $60,000 or higher per year. If you possess an EMT or paramedic certification, then you may receive $100 to $500 every month as incentive bonus. You may enjoy other host of benefits. You can contact the fire department you are interested in to find out more about their benefits.

Start With the Pre-Requisites

Before you apply for the fire service, make sure you meet the requirements. The basic requirements in order to apply for any position at the fire department are:

- You should be 18 years of age or older
- You should hold a high school diploma or a G.E.D.
- You should have a valid driver's license for the state you are applying in

- You should be free from crime and violence because fire departments carry out extensive background investigations on the candidates
- You should be physically and mentally fit
- You should possess some kind of EMT training or certification. In case you don't, you will need to acquire the certification after you are hired.

Sometimes you may also require a residency status, possess good communication skills, ability to perform under extreme pressure, display good sense of judgment, work as a team and also follow instructions from superiors, and be proactive and self-motivated.

Prospective firefighters can also join a local community college to undertake an EMT program. Make sure once you complete the course, you will achieve the credentials that meet the requirements of the fire district where you plan to work. Once you complete the course, you can take the EMT certification offered by National Registry of Emergency Medical Technicians.

If you yearn to be a more desirable candidate, you can attain an associate's or a bachelor's degree. This will help you to move into careers in fire science, paramedics, or leadership roles within fire departments. You can attain a degree in Forestry with a firefighting or environmental focus, which is also available at the bachelor and master's degree levels. Some fire departments also host accredited apprenticeship programs that combine classroom training with field internships. This can take up to four years to complete. To become the most desirable candidate you can attain an associate's or a bachelor's degree studying topics that are relevant to firefighting, such as Chemistry, Math, Biology, Computer Literacy, Communication Skills, etc. You can also earn a degree in fire science or fire protection engineering. You can also enroll in a 2-year Associate of Public Safety and Security degree. This curriculum covers essential courses in terrorism, criminal justice, public administration, administrative law, protection management, dynamics of violence, cyber crime, patrolling, screening, etc. In case you have time, you can just take fire technology classes at the local community college. These courses will help you to better fit in to the firefighting profession. Alternately, you can also become a licensed paramedic.

Practice for the Exam

In this written exam you will find 100 multiple-choice questions. You need to start testing early with any fire department that you qualify for. Every test you take will better prepare you for the next one. Work on your mistakes and weakness. For instance, if you find the math portion of the written exam difficult, work hard to improve your math skills.

Since it is a multiple-choice exam, you have 25% chance to pick the right answer, while you won't get penalized for the wrong choice. Mark your answers properly. In case you want to change your answers later, make sure you erase the wrong option properly before you tick the other one. Don't spend too much time on one question if you are unsure. The firefighter tests typically include memory recall, directional orientation, basic mathematics, mechanical aptitude, judgment and reasoning, and reading comprehension.

Good memory is essential, especially when you are handling emergency situations. You will need to quickly grasp floor plans and exits, fire hose connections and location of fire-suppression systems. This is useful when there is a raging fire and intense smoke. The memory recall section may be the first section in your written test so take it seriously. If you are gifted with photographic memory this section will be your dream. If not, try to form images in your mind that are pertinent to the items you are memorizing and then associate them. Typically you will be given 5 minutes to memorize floor plans, descriptive passages, sketches of emergency scenes, etc. Then your question and answer sheet will follow. Memory recall is an integral part of the entire test.

Get through the Application Process

When fire departments are looking to hire new recruits, they usually participate in recruitment fairs. The hiring process is usually lengthy so maintain some patience. They host screening events where candidates take written and physical tests. If you qualify the first round of tests, you will be interviewed and often go through an additional series of evaluations and testing. Typically, applicants take at least two exams: a written test and a Candidate Physical Ability Test (CPAT) test.

You need to pass the background investigation. This is very crucial to any job at the fire department. You will also need to pass the physiological examination that will demonstrate your ability to handle stress and pressure of your job. You need to also demonstrate effective communication and analytical skills along with courage and motivation.

It is essential you pass the medical exam. In order to become an efficient firefighter, you need to demonstrate high level of physical fitness, agility, coordination and strength.

During the Candidate Physical Ability Test (CPAT), you will be tested rigorously. You will need to demonstrate your agility, speed, endurance and strength. The test includes 8 exercise drills that you have to complete in 10 minutes and 20 seconds or less. You either pass or fail these tests. You will have to wear 50 lb. vest, a hard hat, long pants and other heavy equipment throughout the test.

The written test includes topics such as judgment, communication, problem solving and even memory. You can find helpful exam guides. Most fire departments hire by the exam scores, so it is essential that you have the best score possible.

Successfully Complete the Training

Once you are hired, you will receive intense training at the Fire Academy. This will include both classroom and hands-on training.

Typically, you will require training on emergency medical procedures, fire prevention, firefighting techniques, hazardous materials control, how to handle hazardous materials, learning building codes to give fire inspections, how to carry out rescue operations, etc. Once you successfully complete the training, you will be placed in the fire department. You may or may not receive remuneration for this training but you will receive the title of a professional firefighter once you have passed all the tests and also completed your practical training. Now you are ready to become a working firefighter. You should be proud of yourself and your job.

Going forward make sure you keep updating and honing your skills whenever you can. Depending on your interest areas and the needs of the fire department, you can get First Aid and CPR training, earn a graduate degree in public administration, get EMT or paramedic certification in case you don't have one, get hazardous materials certification, get lifeguard certification, etc. Stay physically fit throughout your tenure at the fire department.

The job of a firefighter is extremely crucial and demanding so make sure you spend sometime at the gym. Observe healthy eating and sleeping habits. Your workout regimen should include strength training.

Chapter 2: Benefits of Becoming a Firefighter in the U.S.

There are many benefits of becoming a Firefighter. It is better you check the benefits for the fire departments you care to join individually. Some fire departments may appeal to you more for better benefits.

Though all the Fire Departments have different incentives, but they will align around the following mostly:

- **Health Insurance**
- **Tuition Fees**
- **Free Training**
- **Retirement and Tax Benefits**
- **Life Insurance**
- **Incentives & Rewards**.

Some Fire Departments also provide low cost home cooked meals, live-in bunkroom accommodation, new turnout gear when you earn a certification and pass the physical test, Gas Card for personal vehicles when you pass firefighter one or two certification and answer at least 15% of the department's alarms, etc. You may also reimburse cost for childcare when you are preparing for the firefighter certifications.

Different Fire Departments also offer different incentives and rewards for the service of the firemen. For instance, Allegheny Mountain Firefighter Initiative offers their members $2,500 Length of Service Award if they earn firefighter two certification during the grant period and fulfill 20 years of service. The SAFER grant offered by the Hyattsville Volunteer Fire Department provides the active members apparel, training and transportation reimbursement, and other tools to help you perform your duties to the maximum level and making an impact. The Fairfax County Volunteer Fire and Rescue Association offers Property tax exemption to members who complete 240 hours of annual service. They can use it to claim tax exemption on one personal vehicle registered in Fairfax County.

Some Fire Departments also provide comprehensive annual physical screening and free immunizations and follow-up care. They can also organize amazing events for the entire fire department community to acknowledge and celebrate accomplishments of the team. The Hyattsville Volunteer Fire Department houses holiday parties, regular firehouse meals, and team building events. They also participate in the hockey team at the DC Firefighters Burn Foundation tournament.

Being a firefighter is a truly rewarding experience by itself. You save lives and also get to be part of a highly dedicated, respectable and a strong community. You work as a close-knit team and always have each other's back. You will make life-long friends here. The satisfaction and confidence you get from being part of this community is inexplicable. The benefits and incentives are added benefits but the true essence of a being a firefighter is love for humanity and for serving others at the cost of his or her own life.

Chapter 3: Advantages and Disadvantages of being a Firefighter in the U.S.

Once you decide to become a firefighter you need to be aware that you may need to fight through tough circumstances sometimes. You may also die trying to save others. The work of a firefighter is not easy, to say the least. It requires a certain level of dedication and commitment towards your job and towards the people of America. In this profession, you may have to risk your own life in order to save the life of others. There is nothing else that should matter to you at that moment, not even your loved ones back home. There is a huge deal of sacrifice you have to live with. You may have to handle emergency situations also. Still this is a satisfying career and deeply rewarding.

When you want to join a fire service, make sure you understand the roles and responsibilities that encompass the job you are interested to apply for. Understand the pros and cons of your job and your role as a firefighter before you finally decide to become a firefighter.

Let us briefly discuss the advantages and disadvantages of becoming a firefighter:

- **You will have to work for a team-centered workplace**
- **You need to meet the minimum educational requirements to apply for a position as a firefighter**
- **You need to be physically fit in order to qualify for the job**
- **Your work schedule may be unpredictable and may require long hours sometimes**
- **The benefits of this profession are immense**
- **You may die in this profession, literally.**

When you join the fire service, you need to start working for the team. You are no more an individual. It is very important that you can work together as a team and not as an individual. You will literally work together with other firefighters to help civilians out of emergencies, such as raging fires or car accidents. So if you don't like to work with a group then this is not the right career choice for you. You have to watch the back of other firefighters too. It is critical that you put others life before yours. You need to protect your team too. Working as a team also means that you will find brotherhood and lifelong friendships prevalent throughout your service at the fire department. Sometimes you need to spend long hours at the fire department with your team so you will eat, sleep and breathe together.

In order to apply for a firefighter position, you need to complete high school at least. However, in some cases if you have a 2-year Fire Science degree, then you stand better chances as a candidate, especially when there is a fierce competition for the same open position. Even to grow in your career in the fire department, advanced degree in fire science can give you an edge.

In order to be in this profession for a longer time, you need to maintain high levels of physical fitness. This is very critical to be efficient in your job at all times. Even when there is no emergency, you need to make sure that all the equipment, fire engines and other emergency vehicles are working properly. You need to spend time testing all the equipment, perform safety drills and make sure supplies are adequate for a sudden emergency. You need to be always prepared for an emergency. These activities will help you to keep up your physical fitness and maintain a certain self-discipline always.

When you are a firefighter, you need to work with emergencies most of the time. So it is usual to have long hours at work. You can have emergencies at any time of the day or night, so you need to be well prepared to cater to it when you have to. Sometimes you may have to work for 24-hour shifts and sometimes even 56 hours a week. Fire departments provide sleeping accommodations also, so you can cater to an emergency immediately. Make sure you are ready to sacrifice your sleep and wake up at any time. Even though you may have to stay away from home a lot, you also get to enjoy time-off a lot. For instance, an average firefighter may work for just 10 full-day shifts a month. This means you get to enjoy the other 20 days with your family and loved ones.

The benefits of joining this profession are immense. An average firefighter receives $ 45,250 or more per year. Many firefighters also receive paid vacation, health insurance, early retirement and pension. You will always find jobs in this profession because we need fire departments, no matter where we live. Due to the increase in population in our country, you may see an increase in the number of emergency calls and jobs on firefighters in the coming years. Due to the immense job security, this profession will always be appealing to fellow Americans.

There are benefits and risks to this profession. You have to understand that you need to save lives, sometimes that would mean to sacrifice your own. We all know that 343 brave firefighters perished when the Twin Towers fell. This is the reality of this profession. Are you willing to sacrifice your own life? This is a very important question you need to ask yourself before you even apply for a firefighter position. Apart from that, there are others risks and injuries, such as burns and smoke, falls, overexertion and even cancer. Firefighters have increasing chances of developing cancer due to the exposure to carcinogens. They are usually exposed to exhaust of fire engines, soot, formaldehyde, benzene, chloroform, styrene, etc. The common forms of cancer are prostate cancer, testicular cancer, non-Hodgkin's lymphoma and multiple myeloma. Even while working at the fire station, it is common to inhale carcinogenic chemicals.

A fireman also has the risk of falls, burns and smoke, and overexertion. When firefighters enter a burning building, there are chances that the building may collapse. In such cases, the fireman may fall along with it. Even when they need to rescue victims from raging fires, they may hurt themselves severely. Falling from the ladder may also cause broken bones. When a fireman enters a burning building to rescue trapped people, they themselves are at risk of getting burnt. The smoke can also be fatal sometimes. If the equipment fails for some reason, the firefighter is at risk of smoke inhalation. A report from the U.S. Fire Administration claims that direct contact with smoke and fire can cause a total of 34 % of all injuries to firemen. Apart from these, the fireman fights continuously with the weight of his or her own equipment while battling with fire. While thick coats, facemasks and oxygen tanks protect the firefighters, the heavy weight of the equipment overexerts the firemen further while they are desperately trying to save lives. And not to add, they also need to carry ladders, hoses, axes and other firefighting equipment to fight the blaze. A report from the U.S. Fire Administration claims that overexertion can cause a total of 25 % of all injuries to firemen.

Chapter 4: Quick 10 Things To Know Before becoming a Firefighter in the U.S.

As a profession, it is not easy to be a firefighter. You can have some real tough competition and the hiring process can also be challenging. You will require a strong will to make it through. Studies show that 70% give up this profession for another career choice because they don't realize what they are getting into earlier.

If you are serious about making it through the hiring process, make sure you are well adept and qualified for the position. The best ways to improve your chances are:

- **Understand the recruitment process**

To successfully pass the hiring process and to become a firefighter, you need to first understand the recruitment process well so that you can prepare accordingly. Learn about each step of the hiring process. Find out the different phases of the recruitment process, such as oral interview, written test, background investigation, physical fitness test, etc. Do some research online and also find out about how the different fire departments around you conduct their recruitments.

- **Be an Emergency Medical Technician (EMT)**

Most of the fire departments require EMT-certified professionals to hire as a firefighter. Almost 90% will require that you complete the certification as soon as you are hired. As a firefighter you need to report to medical-related responses almost 70% of the time. Fire departments look for licenses paramedics so that way they don't need to offer you too much training. You can also get some experience as an EMT on a 9-1-1 ambulance. If you want to consider becoming a firefighter, try to join EMT classes or join a Paramedic school. But don't do it just to increase your chances in the hiring process. Do it only if you are genuinely interested to work as an EMT or Paramedic.

- **Volunteer for community service**

The job of a firefighter is all about saving lives. You can gather more experience even in a non-firefighter role. You can try to volunteer for community service to help build your resume. You can also gather references. When you start doing community service in a non-fire related area, you will start understanding the essence of your role and the satisfaction you will receive when you save lives and make others smile. Try to join The American Red Cross. You can also meet and start networking with other fire service professionals during burn camps. Try to make an impact on your community by joining homeless shelters, big brother programs, habitat for humanity, etc. When you join a fire service, you will want to be someone with a diverse background and experience with serving people.

- **Stay out of trouble**

Make sure you stay away from trouble and crime if you seriously consider becoming a firefighter. You will go through a background investigation on your profile. So keep it as clean as possible. No traffic tickets, vehicle accidents, domestic violence, conviction, anger management issues, drug charges, etc. are allowed. Even if you cannot change your past completely, but try to change it for the better as soon as possible. You don't want your past to haunt you for long.

- **Sign up for fire technology classes**

If possible try to enroll for fire technology classes at a local community college. It will show your dedication and commitment towards your career. You can take classes on the more critical areas like building construction and fire behavior. When you undergo training after you are hired you will receive only 3 to 5 hours of class on each area whereas, when you join a community college you can learn about them for 53 hours or so, which is a huge benefit for you after you become a firefighter. Also, it will provide an edge to your resume.

- **Keep all your records ready**

Be aware that your profile will be sent for background investigation. So make sure all your records are ready and up-to-date. Don't lie to your recruiter. They will find out anyway! The background investigation packet is usually 25 pages long. It will ask you personal questions. You may do well in the test but if you lie here, you will lose the job. You may have to answer questions regarding your academic background, college transcripts, previous employment information, family details, driving record, credit card history, military experience, proof of identity, etc. Some of the typical questions could be:

1. Provide complete information regarding your previous employment (dates, title, duties, salary, supervisor name, etc.).
2. Provide complete information regarding all the high schools and colleges you have attended (they can ask about your

grades, dates attended, degrees received, etc.).

3. Provide information regarding your family members and friends. The background investigator may use this information to contact your close ones to ask about you.

4. Provide information regarding your credit history and other bank accounts held (they can ask about your credit score, bank account balance, etc.). Keep in mind that a bad credit score can hurt your background investigation.

5. Provide information regarding your driving record, traffic tickets, accidents, etc.

6. Provide information regarding any military experience.

Be precise. Be honest. They can also ask photocopies of key documents, licenses, certificates, etc. Keep all the information ready because you will have about a week or less to complete it and send it back. If you waste time waiting to get your transcripts while filling up the form, you may miss out on the deadline and lose the job.

- **Maintain self-discipline**

Becoming a firefighter is not easy. You need to maintain self-discipline too. So start doing your own tasks by yourself. Start with simple tasks at home, such as cleaning your laundry, cleaning the bathroom and toilet, scrubbing your dishes, cooking your meal, etc. Your team at the fire department will not want to teach your these duties. Your training will be more hands-on experience on building construction, fire behavior, equipment and tool operations and maintenance, etc. You need to start being independent so that you can take over more important duties once you join the fire service.

- **Learn about fire-fighters at the fire stations**

If you want to become a firefighter, find out more about their lives. To become one, you need to understand their lifestyle, dedication, perseverance, duty, etc. If there is any particular fire station you are interested in, visit the station. Since firefighters have gone through the hiring process themselves, it will like hearing from the horse's mouth. Ask questions, look around and gather information and knowledge. This will help you prepare better for any firefighter position you are preparing for, and also for the interviews. You may be asked questions such as, "Why do you want to work for this fire department?" When you visit the particular fire department, you can use real time knowledge and experience to help strengthen your response. You can talk about how you met the firefighters in that fire department and you were inspired by their motivation and experience. You can talk about your unique story that will emphasize more about your zeal and enthusiasm about joining that fire department.

- **Practice taking the tests**

Start taking the firefighter tests today. This is the best way to understand the different phases of the hiring process. This way you will know what to expect and you can prepare accordingly. Work on your strengths and weakness. Most of the fire departments have similar hiring process so it will give you a fair idea of how it will be anywhere else. If you make mistakes in your tests, make sure you correct it. Learning from your mistakes is essential if you want to strengthen your candidature. You can start looking for fire service jobs at www.firerecruit.com. This website will help you find firefighter jobs across the United States. You need to be proactive in finding positions that interest you. Also find out about the departments that are conducting tests because some departments conduct these tests infrequently, while others rarely. Some departments may test every 6 months, whereas most departments test every 2-3 years. Some large metropolitan departments may test once in 6-10 years. So an opportunity lost could be grave. You have to take the tests in order to get hired. So look closely for any opportunity to take the test anywhere. You can also subscribe to www.firerecruit.com to make sure you don't lose out on these precious opportunities.

- **Gather knowledge about the firefighter profession online**

Being a firefighter is not easy. You should learn about their lives and understand fully what you are getting into. You should be passionate about it. You can subscribe to fire service publications like FireEngineering magazine, Firehouse Magazine, etc. You can also subscribe to their emails to keep in touch. During your interview you may have to answer to questions, such as "Where do you see yourself in this fire department in 5 years?" or "What challenges do you see in today's fire services?" When you have to answer in-depth questions related to a fire department, it is better you know everything about the department and the role you are pursuing. You need to find opportunities to learn more about the fire service online as you may not find any defined courses. Ask your local firefighters to help you with hands on training and experience whenever possible.

Even though completing all the above suggestions may not guarantee a job with a fire department, but it sure enhances your chances amidst the crowd. As long as you are well informed and determined, your candidature will be hard to miss attention from the hiring committee.

Conclusion

Thank you again for purchasing this book!

I truly hope this book helped you understand how to become a firefighter in the U.S.

Your next step is to understand find out the career opportunities you are interested in a fire department and work towards it using the suggestions mentioned in this book.

Click here to leave a review for this book on Amazon!

Thank you and good luck!

Made in the USA
Las Vegas, NV
09 April 2022

47145031R00024